Reinh

How to receive a Miracle from God

How To Receive A Miracle From God
English
Copyright © Full Flame GmbH 2003
ISBN 3-935057-13-X

Edition 5, Printing 3
50,000 copies

Originally published by CfaN 1992
ISBN 3-9802990-2-3

477,000 copies in print
in 16 languages

Cover design by Isabelle Brasche
Cover photographs by Peter van den Berg and Roland Senkel
Typeset by David Lant

Published by Full Flame GmbH,
Postfach 60 05 95, 60335 Frankfurt am Main,
Germany.
www. fullflame.com

Visit the CfaN web site at www.cfan.org

Printed in China

HOW TO RECEIVE A MIRACLE FROM GOD

MIRACLE TERRITORY

New Testament believers did not go around searching and probing 'to get a miracle.' They lived on miracle territory. They were in the kingdom of God, and they perceived the miracle-working hand of God in every situation. Believers understood everyday-Christianity to be miraculous, miracles through and through. That theme is common in the letters of the apostle Paul.

Regrettably, what was normal then is not normal now. So much emphasis has been placed upon finding new methods for miracles that it sounds as if it were all a profound secret. We need to remove the mystery and get back to the *simplicity that is in Christ* (2 Corinthians 11:3). So, we shall look at a miracle and then see something greater.

THE TEACHING COURSE BEGINS

We begin with a lesson by Christ Himself.

Matthew 14:25-29:

> *Now in the fourth watch of the night Jesus went to them, walking on the sea. And when the disciples saw Him walking on the sea, they were troubled, saying, "It is a ghost!" And they cried out for fear.*
>
> *But immediately Jesus spoke to them, saying, "Be of good cheer! It is I; do not be afraid."*

And Peter answered Him and said, "Lord, if it is You, command me to come to You on the water."

So He said, "Come." And when Peter had come down out of the boat, he walked on the water to go to Jesus.

As we study this, we shall discover three basic elements, or dynamics, of miracles, but first, let us look carefully at the background.

WHERE THE MIRACLE BEGAN

As the disciples crossed the Sea of Galilee at dawn, they saw a human form gliding across the water, silhouetted against the eastern sky. They rubbed their eyes. Was it a hallucination? But it did not go away. It was real, something neither they, nor anyone else, had ever seen. They broke out in a cold sweat and cried out hoarse with terror.

Two minutes later there was further consternation among them. Peter jumped over the side of the boat. What is more, he did not plunge into the water as they had expected, but landed on it as if it were an asphalt road! His feet hit the water with a bump, not a splash. Now there were two figures walking the waves!

TWO IMPORTANT FACTS

1. Miracle conditions began while Peter was still in the boat. Suddenly he became different. One minute panicking, his hair standing on end, and the next minute daring to do what no mere man had ever done - walk on water.

When Peter changed, the situation changed. Peter found things different when he was different. Some people accept things as they are, and then blame what they are on where they are. However, we know that when Christ comes into someone's life, then heaven works things out. Situations can be changed. That is a great biblical truth.

If we look more carefully at the story of Peter, we shall see something even greater than Peter's circumstances changing. Nothing had changed in Peter's environment. The water looked exactly the same. But Peter had changed; he had become master of the circumstances. The sea billows still rolled, but Peter walked over them; he made a doormat of them. Jesus saves us and our households, us and the things around us (Acts 16:31). Miracles begin within us and then affect our surroundings. The sea threatened Peter, opening its foaming mouth to swallow him, but Peter made it an open thoroughfare when Jesus called him to come.

2. It was Christ Himself who put the disciples where they were; He *made his disciples get into the boat and go before him to the other side* (Matthew 14:22). Yet the boat was *tossed by the waves, for the wind was contrary* (Matthew 14:24). So troubles may arise when we are, or even because we are, doing God's explicit will, but we must give God time, and let Him work things together for good (Romans 8:28). Jesus, in fact, was in charge; He had seen them struggling out on the Sea of Galilee when He was up on the hillside (Mark 6:47-48). Do not worry the Lord has good eyesight.

Situations can be changed. That is a great biblical truth.

> God does not guarantee us everlastingly calm seas and prosperous voyages.

God does not guarantee us everlastingly calm seas and prosperous voyages. Even Paul was shipwrecked three times. The disciples were fighting the elements in one of the lumbering boats of their day for the very reason that that was where God wanted them.

Many people feel disillusioned about this very thing. They do what is right and suffer for it. But we need not worry. The trouble, which comes when God puts us where he wants us, is a miracle in the making. The stormy winds of Galilee were the first component for a wonder for Peter and his companions.

We cannot say that all our troubles are in that category. Difficulties do not always indicate we are doing God's will. Sometimes they show we are doing our own wills. We land ourselves with problems. For that matter, *man is born to trouble, as the sparks fly upward* as Eliphaz said to Job (Job 5:7); it is 'natural' in our fallen world. Also there is a devil.

Whether a situation is our fault or not, we all need a miracle sometime or other. Difficulties arise for all of us at times, perhaps in health, occupation, marriage, family, or some other area of our lives. Some people find their sins and failures rattling around behind them, the skeletons getting out of the cupboard! Like the disciples in their boat, we can sit amid waves of worry, conjuring up haunting specters - even Jesus was part of the disciples' fears. They needed a miracle, nothing less would do.

Thank God, He did not intend us to live our lives without miracles. His original plan was that, even after we had done our best, we would still be dependent upon Him to meet our needs. Now we come to the three basics of a miracle.

Dynamic No. 1

WALKING ON THE WORD

Peter suddenly threw off fears like a suit of old clothes. His change in attitude left his friends at the oars gasping in astonishment. This was no mere impulse; it was propulsion. How?

It began with a voice. The voice of the One who is the Word. That voice rang across the lake. It was Jesus, the voice that raised the very dead (Mark 5:22-24, 35-43; Luke 7:11-15, 8:41-56; John 11:1-44). It was the most wonderful sound ever to fall on human ears. He himself was the Word (John 1:1).

This Jesus is the living Word. Referring to the Word many years later, Peter said *you do well to heed as a light that shines in a dark place* (2 Peter 1:19). It transforms men and women (Romans 8:2), strengthening their feeble hands, steadying knees that give way (Isaiah 35:3; Hebrews 12:12), and putting new heart into the disheartened.

If we wish to hear the living Word, then we must turn to the written Word. People ignore Scripture, and merely pick up the latest book to learn some new technique. The Word of God is the first secret. Peter knew Christ's voice, but many people seeking miracles do not know the Word of God.

> If we wish to hear the living Word, then we must turn to the written Word.

Dynamic No. 2

WALKING BY FAITH

Jesus called Peter. His words could have calmed the sea, but instead they calmed Peter, or rather stirred him up. *Be of good cheer! It is I; do not be afraid* (Matthew 14:27). Literally, 'I AM (Greek: ego eimi). Do not have phobia.' Peter looked across the white tops of the waves, and at first Jesus was part of his fear. Then Jesus said *"It is I."* His assurance was carried on the winds. He was Master of it all, and He said, *"It is I."*

Peter heard Jesus. For that matter, so did the other disciples, but they continued to sit in the boat, and did not climb overboard like Peter. Were they waiting for Jesus to do something, since He had put them there? Perhaps they thought, "He told us to take this trip, so we must bow to His will."

So often people take that position. They think the Lord has called them to suffer, to endure some misery, and they have no intention of trying to alter what they conceive to be the will of God. They cite Paul's thorn in the flesh - but Paul sought to have God remove it three times (2 Corinthians 12:7-8).

> Faith defies Fate! Jesus showed us that we can defeat the storm, defeat the devil, overcome evil, and change the world.

Well, neither Peter nor Jesus took that attitude. Peter knew that Jesus could and would change things. Some people may bow passively to Fate, or Kismet, resigned to unalterable Destiny, accepting whatever comes as if heaven had decreed it. That is not

9

> Christ commanded the impossible, and made it possible.

the Christian faith. Faith defies Fate! Jesus showed us that we can defeat the storm, defeat the devil, overcome evil, and change the world. God Himself never changes (Malachi 3:6), but He changes the scenery on the stage of life.

PETER CHALLENGED JESUS TO CHALLENGE HIM

Peter knew Jesus. He asked this figure that was walking on the sea saying, *"It is I,"* for proof of His identity. He was not going to believe any spirit, or any supernatural experience. *Test the spirits, whether they are of God* (1 John 4:1). The devil can operate supernaturally. Jesus had given warnings that Satan wants *to deceive, if possible, even the elect* (Matthew 24:24). The powers of witches, witch doctors, occultists, and others are not in doubt.

But how do we know they are counterfeit? The hallmark of Calvary love is missing. They all fail to deliver anybody from the guilt and power of sin (John 8:36; Romans 8:2). At best they bring a false sense of peace and final terrible disenchantment.

Now, one unique characteristic of Christ was that He commanded the impossible, and made it possible. Peter therefore applied the test. Peter knew that Jesus would only have to order something, and then he, Peter, could do it. He did not shout, "Lord, if it is you, still the storm." Peter made his query personal: *"Lord, if it is You, command me to come to You on the water"* (Matthew 14:28).

He knew that Jesus did not always caress His disciples and cuddle them for comfort, like a mother her children. He had a disturbing way of throwing out challenges to people to rise above themselves. Peter touched the very heart of Christ by challenging Jesus to challenge him. Any presentation of Christ that does not show Him like that is not worth very much; it is a poor picture of Him. Our message is: repent, forsake your sin, believe, and be saved - the miracle of salvation. Because Christ commands us, it can and will happen.

There is a startling twist to our Bible story. It says that the Lord *would have passed them by* (Mark 6:48)! He showed no inclination to still the storm. This was one of those occasions when Jesus had better plans. The Lord wanted to teach His disciples a lesson of active trust, not apathetic submission. He would have walked past them to the shore while they still strained at the oars of their sodden craft, and there would have been no miracle. Did they want it that way? Was that the size of their faith? Jesus was approaching. He knew where they were; He had put them there, and He had a purpose in keeping them there. Would they react properly? Well, one man did.

> Peter touched the very heart of Christ by challenging Jesus to challenge him.

CHANCE OF A MIRACLE

If Jesus, the Lord of miracles, was around, walking miraculously on the water, then Peter was not about to miss the chance. Other miracles could happen. Why let him pass by? Peter certainly did not.

Unfortunately, people do let the Lord of miracles pass by. If there is a Jesus, why live as if there were not? If there is a Father in heaven, why live like orphans? If there is a Savior, why die unsaved? If there is a Healer, why not ask him to heal? If there is an all-sufficient Christ, why scratch and scrape like chickens in a farmyard?

> If things can go wrong, they can go right.

If things can go wrong, they can go right. If the devil can work, so can God. How many people expect it? Faith is for the day of calamity, but that is when some believers stop believing. Their faith only flourishes in glorious meetings. They wear their life jackets on deck, but throw them away when they fall into the sea.

So Peter went in for a miracle. Why not, if God is a God of miracles? Live by faith! That is life as God meant it to be. Miracles come to those who live the way of faith. That is God's grand design for our lives, for us to step out, depending on the Word of God and the power of God to give us miracles. We cannot walk with God without experiencing wonders.

WHAT IS A MIRACLE?

What is a miracle - just a rare event of such great magnitude that it silences critics? Many people do not recognize a miracle when they see one. Christ fed the multitude out of a boy's lunch basket, and then the wise and learned demanded that He show them a miracle (John 6:1-13, 25-30)! Jesus said that people would not believe, even if someone were to rise from the dead (Luke 16:31). The carnal mind is too dulled to receive the things of God but sharp enough to rationalize all the works of God.

Miracle in Scripture is a simple word meaning 'a work of power' - just that. It is not the absurd magic of Roman myth, which our word miracle really signifies. Miracles are things all believers should experience constantly, the power of God at work in our lives 365 miracle-packed days every year, 366 in a leap year.

We do not appreciate how divine some events are. God conceals His hand. He does not sound a trumpet before Him when He makes the grass grow, or when He works for us. Too often we hear Christians relating what the devil has done, as if the devil were a lot more active than the Lord. Maybe Satan's style is more showy to impress us, but God goes to the heart of the matter, which is to satisfy His heart of love.

MIRACLE WATERS

When Peter saw Jesus, he saw a miracle happening. Where He was on the lake - that was the place, miracle waters. As long as Peter sat in the boat, there was no miracle. Peter decided to get into that other area so that there would be a miracle. Peter was not going to pass up this miracle chance.

The just shall live by faith (Romans 1:17). There is a life where trust in God brings His daily wonders. We can cling to our little boats of doubt, and struggle against the elements, or we can step out for God. He will not let us down.

Peter called to Jesus, *"Lord, if it is You, command me to come to You on the water"* (Matthew 14:28). Why should Jesus agree to such a proposal? Why, because that is

> When Peter saw Jesus, he saw a miracle happening.

Jesus. When you cast yourself on Him, it is for a life of wonders. It does not mean that we can stroll across Lake Erie whenever we fancy, instead of taking the ferry, or walk on the ocean out of bravado, or pick up snakes (Mark 16:18) just to put God to the test (Matthew 4:7; Luke 4:12). That kind of presumption is as heathen as fire walking. Jesus would not make bread from stones simply to prove that He could (Matthew 4:1-4; Luke 4:1-4), but He multiplied the loaves, when empty stomachs needed it (Matthew 14:13-21, 15:32; Mark 6:30-44, 8:1-9; Luke 9:10-17). The kingdom of God is open to us. Too many people step over its border with only one nervous foot. Peter went with both feet at once.

THE ENABLING COMMAND

Jesus said just one word: *"COME."* There we have it, the first essential for a miracle: the Word of God. In a way it is true that Peter walked on the water, but from the divine angle he was seen to be walking on the Word of God. He put one foot on 'C,' the next on 'O,' stepped onto the 'M' and then onto the 'E.' It worked! The Word of God made all things, and Peter found the water as stable and solid as dry land. There he was walking up the bigger waves and stepping over the little ones without getting even the soles of his sandals damp. He was possibly drier out of the boat than in it.

"For nothing is impossible with God," said the angel Gabriel to Mary (Luke 1:37). Jesus said, *"All things are possible to him who believes"* (Mark 9:23). The Word of God is safe to believe, and to walk on. Jesus wants to graft that truth into our very characters. He wants to make it second nature for us to believe the Word, and to step out on the Word. We can

do what we would otherwise never attempt, and live lives which demonstrate the Word at every step. If we doubt the Word, we will fail; but when he appears and speaks, fears melt like snow in the sun.

MIRACLE ENVIRONMENT

Those who receive the message of the Gospel are in God's miracle environment gladly. I can safely say that 98 per cent of a divine miracle is the power of the Word of God. God speaks, and that is His way of doing things; he said, *"Let there be light," and there was light* (Genesis 1:3).

Jesus spoke, and demons fled by the legion (Mark 5:1-20), cemeteries were shaken, lepers were cleansed (Matthew 8:2-4; Mark 1:40-44; Luke 5:12-14, 17:11-14), storms were stilled (Matthew 8:18, 23-27; Mark 4:35-41; Luke 8:22-25), and multitudes were fed (Matthew 14:13-21, 15:32; Mark 6:30-44, 8:1-9; Luke 9:10-17). His words disarmed the temple police trying to arrest Him. They said, *"No man ever spoke like this Man"* (John 7:46). He spoke with authority. Let people listen to the preaching of the Word. That is the power pack - the Gospel.

When I first saw the significance of the word *come* spoken by Jesus, I said, "Lord, if I had such a personal word from you as Peter did, I would jump too. But I am living 2,000 years later." At that moment the Holy Spirit whispered in my heart, "Read Matthew 11:28!" I did, and there it was: *"**Come** to Me, all you who labor and are heavy laden, and I will give you rest."*

> The number one dynamic - the Word of God - actually produces number two, the dynamic of faith.

Come *to Me,* **all** *you!* This means everyone, including you and me; no one is excluded. Because Jesus Christ has not changed, nor has the power of His Word, miracles will happen today for all of us. The number one dynamic, the Word of God, actually produces number two, the dynamic of faith. *Faith comes by hearing, and hearing by the word of God* (Romans 10:17).

THE WORD IMPARTS THE POWER TO BELIEVE IN THE WORD

The words of Jesus cause us to trust. They generate their own authority, and carry their own built-in convictions. We can choose to trust them, or not to trust them. We can resist them. That is a matter of choice. Anybody can choose not to believe. Doubt is not a sign of brilliance. Anybody can choose to believe. Faith is a decision; it is a matter of attitude. The Word breathes life into lifeless souls - if they want to live. There is the invitation, *come*, and we can come, striding across the sea if need be, when he bids us.

Peter heard and believed. If he had not, would there have been a miracle? The answer is a resounding no! In fact, the miracle stopped when Peter stopped believing. *But when he saw that the wind was boisterous, he was afraid; and beginning to sink he cried out, saying, "Lord, save me!"* (Matthew 14:30). Of course, Jesus did save him, but that was an anticlimax after such a bold venture of faith.

Having faith is necessary to experience signs and wonders (Mark 16:17-18; Hebrews 11:6). It is a vital part of the miracle circuit. It is faith in Christ Jesus, not just faith in the power of faith, but faith in the power of God. Not faith in ourselves, that we can do this or that, or that something marvelous will happen, but faith in God. Faith is not in miracles, but in Jesus, who makes them happen - and faith means still believing, even when He does not make them happen. He supervises the whole operation, because He is the One who initiated it and involved us by calling us.

This story, somewhat like a parable, has remained with me since my Sunday School days: As a farmer walked across his field, he heard a mouse squeaking. He looked, and a small drama unfolded before his eyes. A snake had hypnotized a mouse; it was paralyzed. All the rodent could do was squeak. The snake edged closer and closer. Then, the story goes, the farmer took out his big handkerchief, and put it between the snake and the mouse. The spell was broken; the mouse could move, and darted away, free.

This might be a children's story, but of one thing I am certain: Many people are paralyzed by a spirit of fear. It is the hypnotic power of *that serpent of old, who is the devil and Satan* (Revelation 20:2). People brood over sickness and death. We listen to medical experts, and begin to tremble and mourn. Fear reduces us to inaction - it prostrates us. The jaws of grief open to devour us.

Then comes the Word of God - God's big 'pocket handkerchief' - let down between us and that hypnotizing, paralyzing, and obsessing terror. The Word of God creates new trust and hope, if we let it. *Therefore if the Son makes you free, you shall be free indeed* (John 8:36).

We may have faith in doctors or other medical experts. They speak within the province of their particular knowledge; they offer only medical opinions, and those can sometimes vary. We can get a second opinion: the Word of God. It is common for medical facts to be interpreted in isolation, out of context to a patient's circumstances. That is not scientific in the truest sense. All facts must be taken into account, and one of those facts is a patient's faith in what the Word of God says.

Faith is believing God more than we believe our feelings, more than our apprehensions. True faith is always in someone - in Jesus, in what He said, is saying, and in what He is doing. People create such difficulties about believing God. Does a child have any difficulty trusting an adult when lifted into his or her arms? Does a four-year-old say, "I don't know whether I have enough faith to let you pick me up"? Children do not have such thoughts, only adults! A child knows nothing about faith, yet exercises it. The more faith we have, the less we notice it. Faith, in the end, is nothing at all; it is just letting God do what He says He will do.

In fact, the first dynamic of a miracle, the Word of God, is 98 per cent of it, and faith is only one per cent. Faith is only the hand by which we take what God offers. That is all that is needed.

The miracle-power circuit is almost closed, but there is one more thing - the remaining one per cent.

Dynamic No. 3

So, Peter heard the word of Jesus, and believed it. But no miracle occurred. Something was missing. What was the missing link?

The last secret is obedience, or action. Peter had to jump overboard. He went overboard for God. He leaped into a miracle.

This explains a lot. It points out a problem that is quite common. Why is it that so many good Christians never personally experience the miracle-working power of God in their lives? They sit so faithfully in their seats at church, listening to the best preachers, even weeping, praying, and confessing, "Lord, I believe." They hear the Word and believe it. Then what? They do not go overboard for God. They just sit there, waiting for Jesus to do something, praying, "Lord, send the power," and He passes by their boats.

If we want things to happen, we must get out of our boats, and move in line with Jesus, walking the waves. He is calling us. He does not say, "Hold tight. I'll soon come across and be with you in the boat." He says, "Come." What, on the water? Yes, that is where the miracles happen.

> If we want things to happen, we must get out of our boats, and move in line with Jesus, walking the waves.

The boat may be just a symbol of our own little ideas. We make them up ourselves. We collect

> Obedience puts the plug in, and the power begins to work. It is the final connection.

them to form 'bits of' creeds, made up of bits of books, bits of sermons, and bits of stories, like birds collecting straw and string to make their nests: "The days of miracles are passed"; "It is God's will for me to be sick because He has something for me to learn." Here is that nest, or that boat. People row these comfortable little boats contentedly for years, believing that eventually they will reach port. They are satisfied to listen to testimonies, or to witness the miracle-working power of God in the lives of others, but if they would go overboard for God, they could walk on the miracle waters themselves.

When Peter went overboard, he rocked the boat. To see God in action we must be in action ourselves, whether we rock the boat or not. Do not worry about the doubters, whom we may disturb. If we are comfortably settled in unchallenging company, where there is no real obedience of faith, then we must jump over the side, right over human opinion, and make for Jesus out there in the miracle waters.

Jump! We *shall not die, but live, and declare the works of the Lord* (Psalm 118:17). The religious thinker and writer Kierkegaard spoke of faith as a leap into the dark, but it is not. It is a leap out of the dark into the light. The blind man leapt out of his darkness into the pool of Siloam, and light broke upon his vision (John 9). The waters will not swallow us, but will carry us, like the waters of the flood, which bore believing Noah, while drowning the whole world of scoffers.

The whitecaps that snarled and roared, dashing Peter's boat, suddenly became horses to carry him on his way to Jesus. Destroy us? Jesus destroyed destruction at the cross. He will not come and carry us piggyback. He smiles, beckons, and says, "Come."

Obedience puts the plug in, and the power begins to work. It is the final connection. Remember what Smith Wigglesworth told a conventional doubting clergyman: "The Acts of the Apostles was written because the apostles acted."

Let us write a few more chapters ourselves!

Other booklets
by REINHARD BONNKE

The Holy Spirit Baptism
The greatest assurance of all flows from personal experience of the manifestation of God's power. Drawing from Scripture, this carefully explained and simple to understand booklet brings the believer to the place of faith where he or she can receive the Baptism of the Holy Spirit. Common misconceptions are answered and the reader is challenged to ask and receive!

• 32 pages
• ISBN 3-935057-12-1

How to have Assurance of Salvation
This booklet tackles the first and most vital crisis that every new believer faces. Before anything else, we must know we are saved! It is the crucial link between salvation and discipleship. Using graphic illustrations from Scripture, this message forms the basis of the booklet Now that You are Saved, given to new believers in every CfaN campaign.

• 28 pages
• ISBN 3-935057-11-3

First of all ... Intercession
"Evangelism without intercession is like an explosive without a detonator," says Reinhard Bonnke. Christians have a world to reclaim and regain for God. Prayer and intercession cast out the entrenched enemy, violate his borders and retake lost territory. This booklet explains the task of intercession clearly and concisely, and encourages Christians to use the weapon of prayer more consistently and effectively.

• 32 pages
• ISBN 3-935057-17-2

The Secret Power of the Blood of Jesus

The blood type of Jesus is unique. Since it was spiritually created it has spiritual power. As a young evangelist Reinhard Bonnke vowed that wherever he went he would preach on the blood of Jesus. This booklet contains that powerful gospel message in all its life-changing anointing.

- 24 pages
- ISBN 3-935057-10-5

The Coming One

Now that we are in the third millennium, millions of people are still looking for a great global leader. They even consult the stars looking for a new age under a super-personality to bring accord between the races, peace among the nations, and the rich caring for the poor. Christ declared that He would come back, and He will! This is the key hope of every Christian creed. The last prayer of the Bible is Amen! Come Lord Jesus!

New!

- 28 pages
- ISBN 3-935057-84-9

The Lord Your Healer

God loves to heal. He still heals today. During CfaN campaigns, we see thousands receive healing and remain totally healed. This straight forward but profound booklet answers the critics and lifts our faith. We do not look to church leaders, special ministries or Reinhard Bonnke for healing, but to Jesus. He will answer.

- 24 pages
- ISBN 3-935057-14-8

The Romance of redeeming Love

When God gave his Son Jesus to die for us, it cost him everything. The gift of Redemption is the ultimate expression of God's love. This booklet reveals through Scripture, God's unique and perfect Redemption plan. Creation was easy, but for our Redemption, God gave himself.

- 32 pages
- ISBN 3-935057-15-6

Faith for the Night

In this booklet Evangelist Reinhard Bonnke explains that faith is like a wiring system that carries power into our lives. Faith itself is not the power, but it links us to the power source. There is no link to God's power without faith!

- 28 pages
- ISBN 3-935057-16-4

For further information about the ministry of Reinhard Bonnke or Christ for all Nations, please visit our web site or contact the office nearest to you;

Christ for all Nations
P.O. 590588
Orlando
FL 32859-0588,
USA

Christ for all Nations
P.O. Box 25057
London, Ontario
N6C 6A8
Canada

info@cfan.org
www.cfan.org

For information about the purchase of other books and booklets by Reinhard Bonnke contact;

Full Flame, LLC
P.O. Box 593647
Orlando, FL 32859
USA

Full Flame, GmbH
Postfach 60 05 95
60335 Frankfurt am Main
Germany

info@fullflameonline.com
www.fullflameonline.com

info@fullflame.com
www.fullflame.com